SONGS OF KABIR

SONGS
OF KABIR

A 15th Century Sufi Literary Classic

Translated by Rabindranath Tagore
Introduction by Andrew Harvey

WEISER BOOKS
Boston, MA/York Beach, ME

First published in 2002 by
Red Wheel/Weiser, LLC
368 Congress Street
Boston, MA 02210
www.redwheelweiser.com

Library of Congress Catalog Card Number: 74-82318
ISBN: 1-57863-249-8

08 07 06 05 04
8 7 6 5 4 3 2

Printed in Canada
TCP

The paper used in this publication meets the minimum
requirements of the American National Standard for
Information Sciences—Permanence of Paper for Printed
Library Materials Z39.48–1992 (R1997).

INTRODUCTION TO
THE 2002 EDITION

YOU have in hand a new edition of a book first published in English in 1915. In this terrible and desperate time—after the terrorist attacks on the World Trade Center and Pentagon permanently shattered a whole civilization's sense of security and began an international war on terrorism that may last for years and decide the future of humanity—it may seem frivolous, even shocking to celebrate the re-publication of a famous translation by Tagore of the Indian mystic Kabir. With human history now being poured red-hot from the cauldron of terror and war, what use is there in reading and meditating on a hundred or so of the poems of an illiterate weaver from Benares? Some five hundred years have passed since Kabir wrote these poems. He lived and worked in a civilization very different from our own and from a mystical vision that may seem irrelevant to us now, trapped as we are in a conflict whose impact is ever more unnerving and brutal.

Kabir wrote, "More than all else do I cherish at heart that love which makes me to live a limitless life in this world?" How in our world, increasingly limited by fear and violence, can we credit his claims let alone believe they have any light to give to our situation?

Such a reaction is understandable but it fails to realize that the root of the problems that now afflict us from every direction lie in a worldwide spiritual crisis that only the highest and deepest mystical knowledge and vision can cure. This worldwide crisis is essentially a crisis of human identity. Humanity as a whole has lost its sense of radical interconnection with the Divine and so with the creation. And, as individuals, we have lost that mystical connection with each other.

More than forty years ago, Teilhard de Chardin wrote, "We have come to the moment when we will have to choose between suicide and adoration." These words may have seemed unduly apocalyptic when they were first written in the 1960s. Now, to anyone who is spiritually awake to what is happening, they are nothing less than the clearest imaginable formulation of the choice that faces humanity. We can choose the suicide of an addiction to materialism and a materialistic vision of humanity or we can choose adoration of the Divine and the Divine in the creation and in the human. Such an adoration could engender a massive revolution of the heart and so a wholly new way of acting in every arena.

Are we as a race going to go on choosing division and separation, the passion to possess and dominate, the constant reaching after violence to solve our problems? Or are we going to listen to the drumbeats of Apocalypse and undergo a vast inner transformation that would at last give us access to the Divine within us and its force, stamina and brilliantly refined knowledge of unity of all beings and things? This is what Kabir wrote of. He called it the "formless God that takes a thousand forms in the eyes of his creatures."

It must be clear now to anyone who wants to see, that the problems the world faces–not only of terrorism but also of environmental holocaust, population explosion and the cruel domination of a world economic system that keeps a few countries living in decadent comfort while the rest of the world starves–cannot be dealt with using the consciousness at which humanity now finds itself. We must transform or commit suicide. We are going to have to take, in massive numbers and with great fervor, a leap into our inner divinity and into the "limitless life in this world" it alone can give us. If we don't do this, not only will we die out as a species, but we're apt to take the whole of Nature with us in a bloodbath of unimaginable devastation and ferocity.

As we struggle–those of us who are awake and many more who will be awakened by the horror of what is to come–the testimony of the greatest mystics

to our essential divine identity and to the powers, new
life, energy, and vision that spring from it will be our
central inspiration. These men and women from his-
tory will be our oxygen, the force and truth that keep
us hoping and fighting and working and enduring
though everything. In the all-testing times ahead,
only a deep mystical inner faith and knowledge will
have the power to lift people to a plane of truth that
no horror or cruelty can disturb.

As we take this new and unprecedented journey
into our divine truth, the hundred or so poems of
Kabir that are offered here in the sublime transla-
tions of Rabindranath Tagore will be of profound
help to us. With Rumi, Jesus, Ramakrishna and
Aurobindo, Kabir is one of a handful of spiritual
geniuses whose realization transcends all barriers of
dogma, religion, country and civilization. Kabir's
God is at once immanent and transcendent and
beyond either. He is both the uncreated Eternal Light
and the cosmos constantly birthed and re-birthed
from it. He is the eternal and glorious One and the
friend directly knowable to all those who want to
offer their hearts in love to Him, whatever their caste
or faith. Only such a clear knowledge is of any use in
the mystical journey for, as he wrote in one of his
greatest poems:

It is a hard fight and a weary one, this fight of the
truth-seeker: for the vow of the truth-seeker is
more hard than that of the warrior, or of the
widowed wife who would follow her husband.
For the warrior fights for a few hours, and the
widow's struggle with death is soon ended:
But the truth seeker's battle goes on day and night,
as long as life lasts it never ceases. (p. 86)

Of Kabir the man, very little is known definitively. He
was born in or around 1398, the son of a Muslim
weaver, Niru, and his wife, Nima, who lived on the
outskirts of India's holiest city, Benares. Kabir's name
is a Muslim one, a Koranic title of Allah meaning
"great," but in the poems of his that have best claim to
authenticity, there is little to suggest that he was a
Muslim in any conventional sense. He criticized
Islam rather than embracing it. He had a sometimes
ferocious contempt for the quibbles and nuances of
Islamic theology. Nor can Kabir be claimed for
Hinduism–he could be just as severe in his mockery
of Hindu beliefs about the status of Brahmins, the
unalterable authority of the Vedas, the necessity of
pilgrimages and worship of idols. There are many leg-
ends of his life that suggest that, by his unconven-
tional behavior, he outraged both the ruling Islamic

authorities and the Brahmins. Like Jesus, he seemed to have the rebel of love's supreme gift of annoying everyone.

Many modern scholars believe that Kabir's radical genius was so threatening to his Hindu contemporaries that they concocted a false legend of him being the "disciple" of the great contemporary Hindu reformer, Ramananda. In the famous old story, Kabir as a boy "knew" that Ramananda was destined to be his master, although he was a Muslim and Ramananda a Brahmin. One day when Ramananda was coming down to bathe in the Ganges, Kabir contrived to hide himself on one of the steps along his path. Unwittingly, Ramanda placed his foot on the boy and cried out "Ram! Ram!" This was the name of the divine incarnation he worshipped. Kabir then sprang up and claimed that this constituted an initiation on Ramananda's part. Ramananda was so moved by his sincerity that he accepted him and taught him the truth of his eternal identity with God.

The only problem with this story is that it probably didn't happen at all and was fabricated as part of a Hindu plot to contain Kabir's wild and direct genius within the conventional patterns of Hindu "master-disciple" relationship. In truth, however, Kabir's realization was self-born and unmediated.

The "guru" he mentions in his poetry is not the external master, but the inner divine voice and guidance. Kabir's whole path is a revolutionary one of direct access to God in the core of ordinary life–one that implicitly critiques and implodes two millennia of conventional Hindu practice.

There is one legend, though, that I would like to believe because it acidly presents Kabir's transcendence of all religion and dogma. In his last years, Kabir retired from Benares to live in the small town of Magahar, some miles to the north, near Gorakhpur. He may have moved there either because he had offended the Islamic authorities of Benares or because he wanted to affront pious Hindu sensibilities that considered Magahar as unholy as Benares was holy (Kabir in many of his poems mocks superstitious "man-made" distinctions). Whatever the reasons for his move, he died in Magahar, probably in the 1470s. His death, it is said, was witnessed by great crowds of people, among whom could be found equal numbers of Hindus and Muslims. When he at last passed away, these two camps set upon each other, each battling to lay claim to his body. Their struggle was as useless as it was absurd. After fighting one another to get to the corpse, they found instead two piles of flowers. A voice from Heaven–

Kabir himself?–told the Muslims to bury one pile according to their religious customs and the Hindus to cremate the other pile according to theirs. It is easy to imagine the irony in that "heavenly voice" since both the Muslims and Hindus so avid to claim him as one of their own on his deathbed had so harried and misunderstood him in life.

The universality, directness, and radicalism of his message that caused Kabir so much pain and trouble during his lifetime is precisely what makes him indispensable to us now. In a world ravaged by the strife between fundamentalist versions of the Divine, it has never been more important for human beings to dare to listen to the simplicity of Kabir, a simplicity that cuts finally through all barriers and distinctions.

> O Servant, where dost thou seek Me?
> Lo! I am beside thee.
> I am neither in temple nor in mosque: I am neither in Kaaba nor in Kailash:
> Neither am I in rites and ceremonies, nor in Yoga and renunciation
> If thou art a true seeker, thou shalt at once see Me: thou shalt meet Me in a moment of time.
> Kabir says, "O Sadhu! God is the breath of all breath." (p. 45)

O friend! hope for Him whilst you live, know whilst
you live, understand whilst you live: for in life
deliverance abides.
If your bonds be not broken whilst living, what hope
of deliverance in death? (p. 46)

I laugh when I hear that the fish in the water are
thirsty:
You do not see that the Real is in your home, and
you wander from forest to forest listlessly!
(p. 91)

Kabir's challenge to all of us–to go beyond all barri-
ers of religion or belief or dogma and plunge here
and now in the core of our lives into a passionate
relationship with the Beloved, within and without,
through adoration and service to others–mirrors
exactly that of Jesus in Logion 3 of the Gospel of
Thomas:

If those who lead you say to you "see the kingdom
is in the sky" then the birds of the sky will precede
you. If they say to you "It is in the sea" then the fish
of the sea will precede you; Rather the Kingdom is
inside you and outside you. When you come to
know yourselves, then you will become known and

you will realize that it is you who are the sons and daughters of the living Father. But if you will not know yourselves, you dwell in poverty, and it is you who are that poverty.

Kabir's and Jesus' great promises to those who are brave enough to see through the versions of God that place the divine in a transcendent beyond is that coming to "know yourself" results in a wholly different life here on earth, one infused at every level with divine passion, knowledge and love.

Kabir came to live this life not as a monk in a monastery or a hermitage, but as a husband, father, and weaver in a tiny shop in an alleyway in Benares. This fact is crucial for all of us who need to know how to live in the divine in the core of a burning world. As he wrote, "Kabir says: the home is the abiding place; in the home is reality; the home helps to attain Him Who is real. So stay where you are, and all things will come to you in time." (p.88)

Again and again, with ruthless wit and tremendous passion, Kabir tells us that it is not necessary to run from the world or go on ceaseless pilgrimages or in fact indulge in any of the sometimes ascetic and life denying disciplines that the religions and mystical transmissions systems have decreed as essential to the true and holy life. What is essential is to wake up to the living presence of God in and as life itself and as the love and power constantly re-inventing all creation, and to live in that sacred knowledge and bliss, radiating the power of that truth through all one's actions and choices. All things are holy when seen with the eyes of awak-ened love. Nothing less than this all-embracing vision of God and divine humanity will bring about the great transformation that is humanity's last and greatest hope.

If we are going to do everything in our power to preserve this planet, it will not be, I believe, in the name of some heavenly ideal nor in the name, cer-tainly, of any one religion or even of a noble polit-ical vision of democracy. Rather, it will be because more and more of us have dared to take the mystic journey into the heart of life and to find what Jesus and Rumi and Kabir and Ramakrishna and Aurobindo and countless others have found there–the living divine fire creating and illuminat-ing and inspiring all things, "the love that makes me to live a limitless life in this world." And with the living and growing experience of that fire and love to fuel all of our struggles and efforts, to give us passion and wisdom, true holy detachment and compassion, there is nothing, even at this late hour, that will be impossible for us.

In time, a tremendous paradox may well be revealed to us—that what we are experiencing now as a time of death is secretly a time of birth and that the crises that now seem insuperable will, in the end, occasion in us a transformation that will at last bring us into the glory of that simple union with the Divine. No other poet has sung of this with so precise a radiance as Kabir:

> O Sadhu! the simple union is the best.
> Since the day when I met with my Lord, there has
>   been no end the sport of our love.
> I shut not my eyes, I close not my ears, I do not
>   mortify my body;
> I see with eyes open and smile, and behold His
>   beauty everywhere:
> I utter His Name and whatever I see, it reminds me
>   of Him; whatever I do, it becomes His worship.
>   (p. 88)

—Andrew Harvey
February, 2002

SONGS OF KABIR

INTRODUCTION

THE poet Kabīr, a selection from whose songs is here for the first time offered to English readers, is one of the most interesting personalities in the history of Indian mysticism. Born in or near Benares, of Mohammedan parents, and probably about the year 1440, he became in early life a disciple of the celebrated Hindu ascetic Rāmānanda. Rāmānanda had brought to Northern India the religious revival which Rāmānuja, the great twelfth-century reformer of Brāhmanism, had initiated in the South. This revival was in part a reaction against the increasing formalism of the orthodox cult, in part an assertion of the demands of the heart as against

the intense intellectualism of the Ve-
dānta philosophy, the exaggerated
monism which that philosophy pro-
claimed.   It took in Rāmānuja's
preaching the form of an ardent per-
sonal devotion to the God Vishnu, as
representing the personal aspect of the
Divine Nature: that mystical "reli-
gion of love" which everywhere makes
its appearance at a certain level of
spiritual culture, and which creeds and
philosophies are powerless to kill.

Though such a devotion is indige-
nous in Hinduism, and finds expression
in many passages of the Bhagavad
Gītā, there was in its mediæval re-
vival a large element of syncretism.
Rāmānanda, through whom its spirit is
said to have reached Kabīr, appears to
have been a man of wide religious cul-
ture, and full of missionary enthusiasm.
Living at the moment in which the
impassioned poetry and deep philoso-

phy of the great Persian mystics, Attār,
Sādī, Jalālu'ddīn Rūmī, and Hāfiz,
were exercising a powerful influence
on the religious thought of India, he
dreamed of reconciling this intense
and personal Mohammedan mysticism
with the traditional theology of Brāh-
manism. Some have regarded both
these great religious leaders as influ-
enced also by Christian thought and
life: but as this is a point upon which
competent authorities hold widely di-
vergent views, its discussion is not at-
tempted here. We may safely assert,
however, that in their teachings, two
— perhaps three — apparently antag-
onistic streams of intense spiritual
culture met, as Jewish and Hellenistic
thought met in the early Christian
Church: and it is one of the outstand-
ing characteristics of Kabīr's genius
that he was able in his poems to fuse
them into one.

A great religious reformer, the
founder of a sect to which nearly a
million northern Hindus still belong,
it is yet supremely as a mystical poet
that Kabīr lives for us. His fate has
been that of many revealers of Reality.
A hater of religious exclusivism, and
seeking above all things to initiate men
into the liberty of the children of God,
his followers have honoured his mem-
ory by re-erecting in a new place the
barriers which he laboured to cast
down. But his wonderful songs sur-
vive, the spontaneous expressions of
his vision and his love; and it is by
these, not by the didactic teachings
associated with his name, that he makes
his immortal appeal to the heart. In
these poems a wide range of mystical
emotion is brought into play : from the
loftiest abstractions, the most other-
worldly passion for the Infinite, to the
most intimate and personal realiza-

tion of God, expressed in homely metaphors and religious symbols drawn indifferently from Hindu and Mohammedan belief. It is impossible to say of their author that he was Brāhman or Sūfī, Vedāntist or Vaishnavite. He is, as he says himself, "at once the child of Allah and of Rām." That Supreme Spirit; Whom he knew and adored, and to Whose joyous friendship he sought to induct the souls of other men, transcended whilst He included all metaphysical categories, all credal definitions; yet each contributed something to the description of that Infinite and Simple Totality Who revealed Himself, according to their measure, to the faithful lovers of all creeds.

Kabīr's story is surrounded by contradictory legends, on none of which reliance can be placed. Some of these emanate from a Hindu, some from a

Mohammedan source, and claim him by turns as a Sūfī and a Brāhman saint. His name, however, is practically a conclusive proof of Moslem ancestry: and the most probable tale is that which represents him as the actual or adopted child of a Mohammedan weaver of Benares, the city in which the chief events of his life took place.

In fifteenth-century Benares the syncretistic tendencies of Bhakti religion had reached full development. Sūfīs and Brāhmans appear to have met in disputation: the most spiritual members of both creeds frequenting the teachings of Rāmānanda, whose reputation was then at its height. The boy Kabīr, in whom the religious passion was innate, saw in Rāmānanda his destined teacher; but knew how slight were the chances that a Hindu guru would accept a Mohammedan as disciple. He therefore hid upon the

steps of the river Ganges, where Rāmā-
nanda was accustomed to bathe; with
the result that the master, coming
down to the water, trod upon his body
unexpectedly, and exclaimed in his
astonishment, "Rām! Rām!" — the
name of the incarnation under which he
worshipped God. Kabīr then declared
that he had received the mantra of
initiation from Rāmānanda's lips, and
was by it admitted to discipleship. In
spite of the protests of orthodox Brāh-
mans and Mohammedans, both equally
annoyed by this contempt of theologi-
cal landmarks, he persisted in his
claim; thus exhibiting in action that
very principle of religious synthesis
which Rāmānanda had sought to es-
tablish in thought. Rāmānanda ap-
pears to have accepted him, and
though Mohammedan legends speak
of the famous Sūfī Pīr, Takkī of Jhansī,
as Kabīr's master in later life, the

Hindu saint is the only human teacher
to whom in his songs he acknowledges
indebtedness.

The little that we know of Kabīr's
life contradicts many current ideas
concerning the Oriental mystic. Of
the stages of discipline through which
he passed, the manner in which his
spiritual genius developed, we are com-
pletely ignorant. He seems to have
remained for years the disciple of
Rāmānanda, joining in the theological
and philosophical arguments which his
master held with all the great Mullahs
and Brāhmans of his day; and to
this source we may perhaps trace his
acquaintance with the terms of Hindu
and Sūfī philosophy. He may or may
not have submitted to the traditional
education of the Hindu or the Sūfī
contemplative: it is clear, at any rate,
that he never adopted the life of the
professional ascetic, or retired from the

world in order to devote himself to
bodily mortifications and the exclu-
sive pursuit of the contemplative life.
Side by side with his interior life of
adoration, its artistic expression in
music and words — for he was a skilled
musician as well as a poet — he lived
the sane and diligent life of the Orien-
tal craftsman.   All the legends agree
on this point : that Kabīr was a weaver,
a simple and unlettered man, who
earned his living at the loom.   Like
Paul the tentmaker, Boehme the cob-
bler, Bunyan the tinker, Tersteegen
the ribbon-maker, he knew how to
combine vision and industry; the
work of his hands helped rather than
hindered the impassioned meditation
of his heart.   Hating mere bodily aus-
terities, he was no ascetic, but a mar-
ried man, the father of a family — a
circumstance which Hindu legends of
the monastic type vainly attempt to

conceal or explain — and it was from
out of the heart of the common life
that he sang his rapturous lyrics of
divine love. Here his works corrobo-
rate the traditional story of his life.
Again and again he extols the life of
home, the value and reality of diurnal
existence, with its opportunities for
love and renunciation; pouring con-
tempt upon the professional sanctity
of the Yogi, who "has a great beard
and matted locks, and looks like a
goat," and on all who think it neces-
sary to flee a world pervaded by love,
joy, and beauty — the proper theatre
of man's quest — in order to find that
One Reality Who has "spread His form
of love throughout *all* the world." [1]

It does not need much experience of
ascetic literature to recognize the bold-
ness and originality of this attitude in
such a time and place. From the

[1] Cf. Poems Nos. XXI, XL, XLIII, LXVI, LXXVI.

point of view of orthodox sanctity,
whether Hindu or Mohammedan, Ka-
bīr was plainly a heretic; and his frank
dislike of all institutional religion, all
external observance — which was as
thorough and as intense as that of the
Quakers themselves — completed, so
far as ecclesiastical opinion was con-
cerned, his reputation as a dangerous
man. The "simple union" with Divine
Reality which he perpetually extolled,
as alike the duty and the joy of every
soul, was independent both of ritual
and of bodily austerities; the God
whom he proclaimed was "neither in
Kaaba nor in Kailāsh." Those who
sought Him needed not to go far; for
He awaited discovery everywhere, more
accessible to "the washerwoman and
the carpenter" than to the self-right-
eous holy man.[1] Therefore the whole
apparatus of piety, Hindu and Moslem

[1] Poems I, II, XLI.

alike — the temple and mosque, idol
and holy water, scriptures and priests
— were denounced by this inconven-
iently clear-sighted poet as mere sub-
stitutes for reality; dead things inter-
vening between the soul and its love —

The images are all lifeless, they cannot speak:
    I know, for I have cried aloud to them.
The Purāna and the Korān are mere words:
    lifting up the curtain, I have seen.[1]

This sort of thing cannot be tolerated
by any organized church; and it is
not surprising that Kabīr, having his
head-quarters in Benares, the very
centre of priestly influence, was sub-
jected to considerable persecution. The
well-known legend of the beautiful
courtesan sent by the Brāhmans to
tempt his virtue, and converted, like
the Magdalen, by her sudden encounter
with the initiate of a higher love, pre-
serves the memory of the fear and dis-

[1] Poems XLII, LXV, LXVII.

like with which he was regarded by the ecclesiastical powers. Once at least, after the performance of a supposed miracle of healing, he was brought before the Emperor Sikandar Lodī, and charged with claiming the possession of divine powers. But Sikandar Lodī, a ruler of considerable culture, was tolerant of the eccentricities of saintly persons belonging to his own faith. Kabīr, being of Mohammedan birth, was outside the authority of the Brāhmans, and technically classed with the Sūfīs, to whom great theological latitude was allowed. Therefore, though he was banished in the interests of peace from Benares, his life was spared. This seems to have happened in 1495, when he was nearly sixty years of age; it is the last event in his career of which we have definite knowledge. Thenceforth he appears to have moved about amongst various

cities of northern India, the centre of
a group of disciples; continuing in
exile that life of apostle and poet of
love to which, as he declares in one of
his songs, he was destined "from the
beginning of time." In 1518, an old
man, broken in health, and with hands
so feeble that he could no longer make
the music which he loved, he died at
Maghar near Gorakhpur.

A beautiful legend tells us that after
his death his Mohammedan and Hindu
disciples disputed the possession of
his body; which the Mohammedans
wished to bury, the Hindus to burn.
As they argued together, Kabīr ap-
peared before them, and told them to
lift the shroud and look at that which
lay beneath. They did so, and found
in the place of the corpse a heap of
flowers; half of which were buried by
the Mohammedans at Maghar, and
half carried by the Hindus to the holy

city of Benares to be burned — fitting
conclusion to a life which had made
fragrant the most beautiful doctrines
of two great creeds.

II

The poetry of mysticism might be
defined on the one hand as a tempera-
mental reaction to the vision of Reality:
on the other, as a form of prophecy.
As it is the special vocation of the mys-
tical consciousness to mediate between
two orders, going out in loving adora-
tion towards God and coming home to
tell the secrets of Eternity to other
men; so the artistic self-expression of
this consciousness has also a double
character. It is love-poetry, but love-
poetry which is often written with a
missionary intention.

Kabīr's songs are of this kind: out-
births at once of rapture and of charity.
Written in the popular Hindī, not in

the literary tongue, they were deliber-
ately addressed — like the vernacular
poetry of Jacopone da Todì and
Richard Rolle — to the people rather
than to the professionally religious class;
and all must be struck by the constant
employment in them of imagery drawn
from the common life, the universal
experience.   It is by the simplest meta-
phors, by constant appeals to needs,
passions, relations which all men under-
stand — the bridegroom and bride, the
guru and disciple, the pilgrim, the
farmer, the migrant bird — that he
drives home his intense conviction of
the reality of the soul's intercourse
with the Transcendent.   There are in
his universe no fences between the
"natural" and "supernatural" worlds;
everything is a part of the creative
Play of God, and therefore — even in
its humblest details — capable of re-
vealing the Player's mind.

This willing acceptance of the here-
and-now as a means of representing
supernal realities is a trait common to
the greatest mystics. For them, when
they have achieved at last the true
theopathetic state, all aspects of the
universe possess equal authority as
sacramental declarations of the
Presence of God; and their fearless
employment of homely and physical
symbols — often startling and even
revolting to the unaccustomed taste
— is in direct proportion to the exalta-
tion of their spiritual life. The works
of the great Sūfīs, and amongst the
Christians of Jacopone da Todì, Ruys-
broeck, Boehme, abound in illustra-
tions of this law. Therefore we must
not be surprised to find in Kabīr's
songs — his desperate attempts to com-
municate his ecstasy and persuade
other men to share it — a constant
juxtaposition of concrete and meta-

physical language; swift alternations
between the most intensely anthropo-
morphic, the most subtly philosophical,
ways of apprehending man's commun-
ion with the Divine.   The need for this
alternation, and its entire naturalness
for the mind which employs it, is rooted
in his concept, or vision, of the Nature
of God; and unless we make some at-
tempt to grasp this, we shall not go far
in our understanding of his poems.

Kabīr belongs to that small group of
supreme mystics — amongst whom St.
Augustine, Ruysbroeck, and the Sūfī
poet Jalālu'ddīn Rūmī are perhaps the
chief — who have achieved that which
we might call the synthetic vision of
God.   These have resolved the per-
petual opposition between the personal
and impersonal, the transcendent and
immanent, static and dynamic aspects
of the Divine Nature; between the
Absolute of philosophy and the "sure

true Friend" of devotional religion.
They have done this, not by taking
these apparently incompatible concepts
one after the other; but by ascending
to a height of spiritual intuition at
which they are, as Ruysbroeck said,
"melted and merged in the Unity,"
and perceived as the completing oppo-
sites of a perfect Whole. This pro-
ceeding entails for them — and both
Kabīr and Ruysbroeck expressly ac-
knowledge it — a universe of three
orders: Becoming, Being, and that
which is "More than Being," *i.e.*, God.[1]
God is here felt to be not the final
abstraction, but the one actuality.
He inspires, supports, indeed inhabits,
both the durational, conditioned, finite
world of Becoming and the uncon-
ditioned, non-successional, infinite
world of Being; yet utterly transcends
them both. He is the omnipresent

[1] Nos. VII and XLIX.

Reality, the "All-pervading" within
Whom " the worlds are being told like
beads." In His personal aspect He
is the "beloved Fakīr," teaching and
companioning each soul. Considered
as Immanent Spirit, He is "the Mind
within the mind." But all these are at
best partial aspects of His nature,
mutually corrective : as the Persons in
the Christian doctrine of the Trinity
— to which this theological diagram
bears a striking resemblance — repre-
sent different and compensating experi-
ences of the Divine Unity within which
they are resumed. As Ruysbroeck
discerned a plane of reality upon which
"we can speak no more of Father, Son,
and Holy Spirit, but only of One Being,
the very substance of the Divine Per-
sons"; so Kabīr says that "beyond
both the limited *and* the limitless is
He, the Pure Being." [1]

[1] No. VII.

Brahma, then, is the Ineffable Fact compared with which "the distinction of the Conditioned from the Unconditioned is but a word": at once the utterly transcendent One of Absolutist philosophy, and the personal Lover of the individual soul — "common to all and special to each," as one Christian mystic has it. The need felt by Kabīr for both these ways of describing Reality is a proof of the richness and balance of his spiritual experience; which neither cosmic nor anthropomorphic symbols, taken alone, could express. More absolute than the Absolute, more personal than the human mind, Brahma therefore exceeds whilst He includes all the concepts of philosophy, all the passionate intuitions of the heart. He is the Great Affirmation, the font of energy, the source of life and love, the unique satisfaction of desire. His creative word is the *Om*

or "Everlasting Yea." The negative
philosophy which strips from the Di-
vine Nature all Its attributes and —
defining Him only by that which He is
not — reduces Him to an "Empti-
ness," is abhorrent to this most vital
of poets. Brahma, he says, "may
never be found in abstractions." He
is the One Love who pervades the
world, discerned in His fullness only
by the eyes of love; and those who
know Him thus share, though they
may never tell, the joyous and inef-
fable secret of the universe.[1]

Now Kabīr, achieving this synthesis
between the personal and cosmic as-
pects of the Divine Nature, eludes the
three great dangers which threaten
mystical religion.

First, he escapes the excessive emo-
tionalism, the tendency to an ex-
clusively anthropomorphic devotion,

[1] Nos. VII, XXVI, LXXVI, XC.

which results from an unrestricted cult of Divine Personality, especially under an incarnational form; seen in India in the exaggerations of Krishna worship, in Europe in the sentimental extravagances of certain Christian saints.

Next, he is protected from the soul-destroying conclusions of pure monism, inevitable if its logical implications are pressed home: that is, the identity of substance between God and the soul, with its corollary of the total absorption of that soul in the Being of God as the goal of the spiritual life. For the thorough-going monist the soul, in so far as it is real, is substantially identical with God; and the true object of existence is the making patent of this latent identity, the realization which finds expression in the Vedāntist formula "That art thou." But Kabīr says that Brahma and the creature are

"ever distinct, yet ever united"; that
the wise man knows the spiritual as
well as the material world to "be no
more than His footstool."[1] The soul's
union with Him is a love union, a mut-
ual inhabitation; that essentially dual-
istic relation which all mystical religion
expresses, not a self-mergence which
leaves no place for personality. This
eternal distinction, the mysterious
union-in-separateness of God and the
soul, is a necessary doctrine of all
sane mysticism; for no scheme which
fails to find a place for it can represent
more than a fragment of that soul's
intercourse with the spiritual world.
Its affirmation was one of the distin-
guishing features of the Vaishnavite
reformation preached by Rāmānuja;
the principle of which had descended
through Rāmānanda to Kabīr.

Last, the warmly human and direct

[1] Nos. VII and IX.

apprehension of God as the supreme
Object of love, the soul's comrade,
teacher, and bridegroom, which is so
passionately and frequently expressed
in Kabīr's poems, balances and controls
those abstract tendencies which are in-
herent in the metaphysical side of his
vision of Reality: and prevents it from
degenerating into that sterile worship
of intellectual formulæ which became
the curse of the Vedāntist school.   For
the mere intellectualist, as for the mere
pietist, he has little approbation.[1] Love
is throughout his "absolute sole Lord":
the unique source of the more abundant
life which he enjoys, and the common
factor which unites the finite and infi-
nite worlds. All is soaked in love:
that love which he described in al-
most Johannine language as the
"Form of God." The whole of crea-
tion is the Play of the Eternal Lover;

[1] Cf. especially Nos. LIX, LXVII, LXXV, XC, XCI.

the living, changing, growing expres-
sion of Brahma's love and joy. As
these twin passions preside over the
generation of human life, so "beyond
the mists of pleasure and pain" Kabīr
finds them governing the creative acts
of God. His manifestation is love;
His activity is joy. Creation springs
from one glad act of affirmation: the
Everlasting Yea, perpetually uttered
within the depths of the Divine Na-
ture.[1] In accordance with this con-
cept of the universe as a Love-Game
which eternally goes forward, a progres-
sive manifestation of Brahma — one of
the many notions which he adopted
from the common stock of Hindu reli-
gious ideas, and illuminated by his
poetic genius — movement, rhythm,
perpetual change, forms an integral
part of Kabīr's vision of Reality.
Though the Eternal and Absolute is

[1] Nos. XVII, XXVI, LXXVI, LXXXII.

ever present to his consciousness, yet his concept of the Divine Nature is essentially dynamic. It is by the symbols of motion that he most often tries to convey it to us : as in his constant reference to dancing, or the strangely modern picture of that Eternal Swing of the Universe which is "held by the cords of love." [1]

It is a marked characteristic of mystical literature that the great contemplatives, in their effort to convey to us the nature of their communion with the supersensuous, are inevitably driven to employ some form of sensuous imagery : coarse and inaccurate as they know such imagery to be, even at the best. Our normal human consciousness is so completely committed to dependence on the senses, that the fruits of intuition itself are instinctively referred to them. In that intuition it seems

[1] No. XVI.

to the mystics that all the dim crav-
ings and partial apprehensions of
sense find perfect fulfilment.   Hence
their constant declaration that they *see*
the uncreated light, they *hear* the celes-
tial melody, they *taste* the sweetness
of the Lord, they know an ineffable
fragrance, they feel the very contact of
love.   "Him verily seeing and fully
feeling, Him spiritually hearing and
Him delectably smelling and sweetly
swallowing," as Julian of Norwich has
it.   In those amongst them who de-
velop psycho-sensorial automatisms,
these parallels between sense and spirit
may present themselves to conscious-
ness in the form of hallucinations : as
the light seen by Suso, the music heard
by Rolle, the celestial perfumes which
filled St. Catherine of Siena's cell, the
physical wounds felt by St. Francis
and St. Teresa.   These are excessive
dramatizations of the symbolism under

which the mystic tends instinctively
to represent his spiritual intuition to
the surface consciousness. Here, in
the special sense-perception which he
feels to be most expressive of Reality,
his peculiar idiosyncrasies come out.

Now Kabīr, as we might expect in
one whose reactions to the spiritual
order were so wide and various, uses
by turn all the symbols of sense. He
tells us that he has "seen without
sight" the effulgence of Brahma, tasted
the divine nectar, felt the ecstatic con-
tact of Reality, smelt the fragrance of
the heavenly flowers. But he was
essentially a poet and musician:
rhythm and harmony were to him the
garments of beauty and truth. Hence
in his lyrics he shows himself to be,
like Richard Rolle, above all things a
musical mystic. Creation, he says
again and again, is full of music: it *is*
music. At the heart of the Universe

"white music is blossoming": love
weaves the melody, whilst renunciation
beats the time.   It can be heard in the
home as well as in the heavens; dis-
cerned by the ears of common men as
well as by the trained senses of the
ascetic.   Moreover, the body of every
man is a lyre on which Brahma, "the
source of all music," plays.   Every-
where Kabīr discerns the "Unstruck
Music of the Infinite" — that celestial
melody which the angel played to St.
Francis, that ghostly symphony which
filled the soul of Rolle with ecstatic joy.[1]
The one figure which he adopts from
the Hindu Pantheon and constantly
uses, is that of Krishna the Divine
Flute Player.[2]   He sees the supernal
music, too, in its visual embodiment, as
rhythmical movement: that mysteri-
ous dance of the universe before the

[1] Nos. XVII, XVIII, XXXIX, XLI, LIV, LXXVI,
LXXXIII, LXXXIX, XCVII.   [2] Nos. L, LIII, LXVIII.

face of Brahma, which is at once an act of worship and an expression of the infinite rapture of the Immanent God.[1]

Yet in this wide and rapturous vision of the universe Kabīr never loses touch with diurnal existence, never forgets the common life. His feet are firmly planted upon earth; his lofty and passionate apprehensions are perpetually controlled by the activity of a sane and vigorous intellect, by the alert common-sense so often found in persons of real mystical genius. The constant insistence on simplicity and directness, the hatred of all abstractions and philosophizings,[2] the ruthless criticism of external religion: these are amongst his most marked characteristics. God is the Root whence all manifestations, "material" and "spiritual," alike proceed; and God is the only need of

[1] Nos. XXVI, XXXII, LXXVI.
[2] Nos. LXXV, LXXVIII, LXXX, XC.

man — "happiness shall be yours when
you come to the Root." [1]   Hence to
those who keep their eye on the "one
thing needful," denominations, creeds,
ceremonies, the conclusions of philos-
ophy, the disciplines of asceticism, are
matters of comparative indifference.
They represent merely the different
angles from which the soul may ap-
proach that simple union with Brahma
which is its goal; and are useful only
in so far as they contribute to this
consummation. So thorough-going is
Kabīr's eclecticism, that he seems by
turns Vedāntist and Vaishnavite, Pan-
theist and Transcendentalist, Brāhman
and Sūfī. In the effort to tell the
truth about that ineffable apprehension,
so vast and yet so near, which controls
his life, he seizes and twines together
— as he might have woven together
contrasting threads upon his loom —

[1] No. LXXX.

symbols and ideas drawn from the most violent and conflicting philosophies and faiths. All are needed, if he is ever to suggest the character of that One whom the Upanishad called "the Sun-coloured Being who is beyond this Darkness": as all the colours of the spectrum are needed if we would demonstrate the simple richness of white light. In thus adapting traditional materials to his own use he follows a method common amongst the mystics; who seldom exhibit any special love for originality of form. They will pour their wine into almost any vessel that comes to hand: generally using by preference — and lifting to new levels of beauty and significance — the religious or philosophic formulæ current in their own day. Thus we find that some of Kabīr's finest poems have as their subjects the commonplaces of Hindu philosophy and religion: the

Līlā or Sport of God, the Ocean of
Bliss, the Bird of the Soul, Māyā, the
Hundred-petalled Lotus, and the
"Formless Form." Many, again, are
soaked in Sūfī imagery and feeling.
Others use as their material the ordi-
nary surroundings and incidents of
Indian life: the temple bells, the cere-
mony of the lamps, marriage, suttee,
pilgrimage, the characters of the
seasons; all felt by him in their
mystical aspect, as sacraments of the
soul's relation with Brahma. In many
of these a particularly beautiful and
intimate feeling for Nature is shown.[1]

In the collection of songs here trans-
lated there will be found examples which
illustrate nearly every aspect of Kabīr's
thought, and all the fluctuations of
the mystic's emotion: the ecstasy, the
despair, the still beatitude, the eager
self-devotion, the flashes of wide illumi-

[1] Nos. XV, XXIII, LXVII, LXXXVII, XCVIII.

nation, the moments of intimate love. His wide and deep vision of the universe, the "Eternal Sport" of creation (LXXXII), the worlds being "told like beads" within the Being of God (XIV, XVI, XVII, LXXVI), is here seen balanced by his lovely and delicate sense of intimate communion with the Divine Friend, Lover, Teacher of the soul (X, XI, XXIII, XXXV, LI, LXXXV, LXXXVI, LXXXVIII, XCII, XCIII; above all, the beautiful poem XXXIV). As these apparently paradoxical views of Reality are resolved in Brāhma, so all other opposites are reconciled in Him: bondage and liberty, love and renunciation, pleasure and pain (XVII, XXV, XL, LXXXIX). Union with Him is the one thing that matters to the soul, its destiny and its need (LI, LII, LIV, LXX, LXXIV, XCIII, XCVI); and this union, this discovery of God, is the simplest and most natural

of all things, if we would but grasp it
(XLI, XLVI, LVI, LXXII, LXXVI,
LXXVIII, XCVII).   The union, how-
ever, is brought about by love, not by
knowledge or ceremonial observances
(XXXVIII, LIV, LV, LIX, XCI);
and the apprehension which that union
confers is ineffable — "neither This
nor That," as Ruysbroeck has it (IX,
XLVI, LXXVI).   Real worship and
communion is in Spirit and in Truth
(XL, XLI, LVI, LXIII, LXV, LXX),
therefore idolatry is an insult to the
Divine Lover (XLII, LXIX) and the
devices of professional sanctity are
useless apart from charity and purity
of soul (LIV, LXV, LXVI).   Since all
things, and especially the heart of
man, are God-inhabited, God-possessed
(XXVI, LVI, LXXVI, LXXXIX,
XCVII), He may best be found in the
here-and-now: in the normal, human,
bodily existence, the "mud" of material

life (III, IV, VI, XXI, XXXIX, XL,
XLIII, XLVIII, LXXII). "We can
reach the goal without crossing the
road" (LXXVI) — not the cloister but
the home is the proper theatre of man's
efforts: and if he cannot find God
there, he need not hope for success by
going farther afield. "In the home is
reality." There love and detachment,
bondage and freedom, joy and pain play
by turns upon the soul; and it is from
their conflict that the Unstruck Music
of the Infinite proceeds. "Kabīr says:
None but Brahma can evoke its
melodies."

III

This version of Kabīr's songs is
chiefly the work of Mr. Rabīndranāth
Tagore, the trend of whose mystical
genius makes him — as all who read
these poems will see — a peculiarly
sympathetic interpreter of Kabīr's

vision and thought. It has been based upon the printed Hindī text with Bengali translation of Mr. Kshiti Mohan Sen; who has gathered from many sources — sometimes from books and manuscripts, sometimes from the lips of wandering ascetics and minstrels — a large collection of poems and hymns to which Kabīr's name is attached, and carefully sifted the authentic songs from the many spurious works now attributed to him. These painstaking labours alone have made the present undertaking possible.

We have also had before us a manuscript English translation of 116 songs made by Mr. Ajit Kumār Chakravarty from Mr. Kshiti Mohan Sen's text, and a prose essay upon Kabīr from the same hand. From these we have derived great assistance. A considerable number of readings from the translation have been adopted by us;

whilst several of the facts mentioned in the essay have been incorporated into this introduction. Our most grateful thanks are due to Mr. Ajit Kumār Chakravarty for the extremely generous and unselfish manner in which he has placed his work at our disposal.

E. U.

The reference of the headlines of the poems is to:

Śāntiniketana; Kabīr by Śrī Kshitimohan Sen, 4 parts, Brahmacharyāśrama, Bolpur, 1910–1911.

For some assistance in normalizing the transliteration we are indebted to Professor J. F. Blumhardt.

Sir Rabindranath Tagore
From a Drawing by W. Rothenstein

KABIR'S POEMS

I

I. 13. *mo ko kahān ḍhūnṛo bande*

O SERVANT, where dost thou
seek Me?

Lo! I am beside thee.

I am neither in temple nor in mosque:
I am neither in Kaaba nor in
Kailash:

Neither am I in rites and ceremonies,
nor in Yoga and renunciation.

If thou art a true seeker, thou shalt at
once see Me: thou shalt meet Me
in a moment of time.

Kabir says, "O Sadhu! God is the
breath of all breath."

II

I. 16. *Santan jāt na pūcho nirguṇiyāṅ*

IT is needless to ask of a saint the
caste to which he belongs;

45

For the priest, the warrior, the trades-
     man, and all the thirty-six castes,
     alike are seeking for God.

It is but folly to ask what the caste of
     a saint may be;

The barber has sought God, the washer-
     woman, and the carpenter —

Even Raidas was a seeker after God.

The Rishi Swapacha was a tanner by
     caste.

Hindus   and   Moslems   alike   have
     achieved that End, where remains
     no mark of distinction.

III

I. 57.   *sādho bhāī, jīvat hī karo āsá*

O FRIEND! hope for Him whilst
     you live, know whilst you live,
     understand whilst you live: for
     in life deliverance abides.

If your bonds be not broken whilst
     living, what hope of deliverance
     in death?

It is but an empty dream, that the soul
>   shall have union with Him because
>   it has passed from the body :
If He is found now, He is found then,
If not, we do but go to dwell in the City
>   of Death.
If you have union now, you shall have
>   it hereafter.
Bathe in the truth, know the true Guru,
>   have faith in the true Name !
Kabir says : "It is the Spirit of the
>   quest which helps ; I am the slave
>   of this Spirit of the quest."

IV

I. 58. *bāgo nā jā re nā jā*

DO not go to the garden of flowers !
>   O Friend ! go not there ;
In your body is the garden of flowers.
Take your seat on the thousand petals
>   of the lotus, and there gaze on the
>   Infinite Beauty.

V

I. 63. *avadhū, māyā tajī na jāy*

TELL me, Brother, how can I re-
 nounce Maya?

When I gave up the tying of ribbons,
 still I tied my garment about me:

When I gave up tying my garment,
 still I covered my body in its folds.

So, when I give up passion, I see that
 anger remains;

And when I renounce anger, greed is
 with me still;

And when greed is vanquished, pride
 and vainglory remain;

When the mind is detached and casts
 Maya away, still it clings to the
 letter.

Kabir says, "Listen to me, dear Sadhu!
 the true path is rarely found."

VI

I. 83. *candā jhalkai yahi ghaṭ māhīn*

THE moon shines in my body, but
my blind eyes cannot see it:
The moon is within me, and so is the
sun.
The unstruck drum of Eternity is
sounded within me; but my deaf
ears cannot hear it.

So long as man clamours for the *I* and
the *Mine*, his works are as naught:
When all love of the *I* and the *Mine* is
dead, then the work of the Lord
is done.
For work has no other aim than the
getting of knowledge:
When that comes, then work is put
away.

The flower blooms for the fruit: when
the fruit comes, the flower withers.

The musk is in the deer, but it seeks it
    not within itself: it wanders in
    quest of grass.

VII

I. 85. *Sādho, Brahm alakh lakhāyā*

WHEN He Himself reveals Him-
    self, Brahma brings into mani-
    festation That which can never be
    seen.

As the seed is in the plant, as the shade
    is in the tree, as the void is in the
    sky, as infinite forms are in the
    void —

So from beyond the Infinite, the Infi-
    nite comes; and from the Infinite
    the finite extends.

The creature is in Brahma, and Brahma
    is in the creature: they are ever
    distinct, yet ever united.

He Himself is the tree, the seed, and
    the germ.

He Himself is the flower, the fruit, and
the shade.
He Himself is the sun, the light, and
the lighted.
He Himself is Brahma, creature, and
Maya.
He Himself is the manifold form, the
infinite space;
He is the breath, the word, and the
meaning.
He Himself is the limit and the limit-
less: and beyond both the limited
and the limitless is He, the Pure
Being.
He is the Immanent Mind in Brahma
and in the creature.

The Supreme Soul is seen within the
soul,
The Point is seen within the Supreme
Soul,
And within the Point, the reflection is
seen again.

Kabir is blest because he has this
supreme vision!

VIII

I. 101. *is ghaṭ antar bāg bagīce*

WITHIN this earthen vessel are
bowers and groves, and within
it is the Creator:
Within this vessel are the seven oceans
and the unnumbered stars.
The touchstone and the jewel-ap-
praiser are within;
And within this vessel the Eternal
soundeth, and the spring wells up.
Kabir says: "Listen to me, my Friend!
My beloved Lord is within."

IX

I. 104. *aisā lo nahīn taisā lo*

O HOW may I ever express that
secret word?
O how can I say He is not like this, and
He is like that?

If I say that He is within me, the universe is ashamed:
If I say that He is without me, it is falsehood.
He makes the inner and the outer worlds to be indivisibly one;
The conscious and the unconscious, both are His footstools.
He is neither manifest nor hidden, He is neither revealed nor unrevealed:
There are no words to tell that which He is.

X

I. 121. *tohi mori lagan lagāye re phakīr wā*

TO Thee Thou hast drawn my love, O Fakir!
I was sleeping in my own chamber, and Thou didst awaken me; striking me with Thy voice, O Fakir!
I was drowning in the deeps of the

ocean of this world, and Thou
didst save me: upholding me
with Thine arm, O Fakir!
Only one word and no second — and
Thou hast made me tear off all
my bonds, O Fakir!
Kabir says, "Thou hast united Thy
heart to my heart, O Fakir!"

XI

I. 131.   *niś din khelat rahī sakhiyān̲
sang*

I PLAYED day and night with my
comrades, and now I am greatly
afraid.
So high is my Lord's palace, my heart
trembles to mount its stairs: yet
I must not be shy, if I would enjoy
His love.
My heart must cleave to my Lover;
I must withdraw my veil, and
meet Him with all my body:

Mine eyes must perform the ceremony
   of the lamps of love.
Kabir says: "Listen to me, friend: he
   understands who loves. If you
   feel not love's longing for your
   Beloved One, it is vain to adorn
   your body, vain to put unguent
   on your eyelids."

XII

II. 24. *haṃsā, kaho purātan vāt*

TELL me, O Swan, your ancient
   tale.
From what land do you come, O Swan?
   to what shore will you fly?
Where would you take your rest, O
   Swan, and what do you seek?

Even this morning, O Swan, awake,
   arise, follow me!
There is a land where no doubt nor
   sorrow have rule: where the terror
   of Death is no more.

There the woods of spring are a-bloom,
    and the fragrant scent " He is I "
    is borne on the wind:
There the bee of the heart is deeply
    immersed, and desires no other joy.

XIII

II. 37. *aṅgaḍhiyā devā*

O LORD Increate, who will serve
    Thee?
Every votary offers his worship to the
    God of his own creation: each day
    he receives service —
None seek Him, the Perfect: Brahma,
    the Indivisible Lord.
They believe in ten Avatars; but no
    Avatar can be the Infinite Spirit,
    for he suffers the results of his
    deeds:
The Supreme One must be other than
    this.
The Yogi, the Sanyasi, the Ascetics,
    are disputing one with another:

Kabir says, "O brother! he who has
seen that radiance of love, he is
saved."

XIV

II. 56. *dariyā kī lahar dariyāo hai jī*

THE river and its waves are one
surf: where is the difference
between the river and its waves?
When the wave rises, it is the water;
and when it falls, it is the same
water again. Tell me, Sir, where
is the distinction?
Because it has been named as wave,
shall it no longer be considered as
water?

Within the Supreme Brahma, the
worlds are being told like beads:
Look upon that rosary with the eyes of
wisdom.

XV

II. 57.   jānh khelat vasant riturāj

WHERE Spring, the lord of the
   seasons, reigneth, there the
Unstruck Music sounds of itself,
There the streams of light flow in all
   directions ;
Few are the men who can cross to that
   shore !
There, where millions of Krishnas stand
   with hands folded,
Where millions of Vishnus bow their
   heads,
Where millions of Brahmās are reading
   the Vedas,
Where millions of Shivas are lost in
   contemplation,
Where millions of Indras dwell in the sky,
Where the demi-gods and the munis
   are unnumbered,
Where millions of Saraswatis, Goddess
   of Music, play on the vina —

There is my Lord self-revealed: and
the scent of sandal and flowers
dwells in those deeps.

XVI

II. 59.   *jānh cet acet khambh dōū*

BETWEEN the poles of the con-
scious and the unconscious, there
has the mind made a swing:
Thereon hang all beings and all worlds,
and that swing never ceases its
sway.
Millions of beings are there: the sun
and the moon in their courses are
there:
Millions of ages pass, and the swing
goes on.
All swing! the sky and the earth and
the air and the water; and the
Lord Himself taking form:
And the sight of this has made Kabir
a servant.

XVII

II. 61. *grah candra tapan jot varat hai*

THE light of the sun, the moon, and
the stars shines bright:

The melody of love swells forth, and
the rhythm of love's detachment
beats the time.

Day and night, the chorus of music fills
the heavens; and Kabir says

"My Beloved One gleams like the
lightning flash in the sky."

Do you know how the moments per-
form their adoration?

Waving its row of lamps, the universe
sings in worship day and night,

There are the hidden banner and the
secret canopy:

There the sound of the unseen bells is
heard.

Kabir says: "There adoration never
ceases; there the Lord of the Uni-
verse sitteth on His throne."

The whole world does its works and
commits its errors: but few are
the lovers who know the Beloved.
The devout seeker is he who mingles
in his heart the double currents of
love and detachment, like the
mingling of the streams of Ganges
and Jumna;
In his heart the sacred water flows day
and night; and thus the round of
births and deaths is brought to an
end.

Behold what wonderful rest is in the
Supreme Spirit! and he enjoys it,
who makes himself meet for it.
Held by the cords of love, the swing of
the Ocean of Joy sways to and fro;
and a mighty sound breaks forth
in song.
See what a lotus blooms there without
water! and Kabir says
"My heart's bee drinks its nectar."

What a wonderful lotus it is, that
blooms at the heart of the spinning
wheel of the universe! Only a
few pure souls know of its true
delight.
Music is all around it, and there the
heart partakes of the joy of the
Infinite Sea.
Kabir says: "Dive thou into that
Ocean of sweetness: thus let all
errors of life and of death flee
away."

Behold how the thirst of the five senses
is quenched there! and the three
forms of misery are no more!
Kabir says: "It is the sport of the
Unattainable One: look within,
and behold how the moon-beams
of that Hidden One shine in you."

There falls the rhythmic beat of life
and death:

Rapture wells forth, and all space is
  radiant with light.
There the Unstruck Music is sounded;
  it is the music of the love of the
  three worlds.
There millions of lamps of sun and of
  moon are burning;
There the drum beats, and the lover
  swings in play.
There love-songs resound, and light
  rains in showers; and the wor-
  shipper is entranced in the taste
  of the heavenly nectar.
Look upon life and death; there is no
  separation between them,
The right hand and the left hand are
  one and the same.
Kabir says: "There the wise man is
  speechless; for this truth may never
  be found in Vadas or in books."

I have had my Seat on the Self-poised
  One,

I have drunk of the Cup of the In-
   effable,
I have found the Key of the Mystery,
I have reached the Root of Union.
Travelling by no track, I have come
   to the Sorrowless Land: very
   easily has the mercy of the great
   Lord come upon me.
They have sung of Him as infinite and
   unattainable: but I in my medi-
   tations have seen Him without
   sight.
That is indeed the sorrowless land, and
   none know the path that leads
   there:
Only he who is on that path has surely
   transcended all sorrow.
Wonderful is that land of rest, to which
   no merit can win;
It is the wise who has seen it, it is the
   wise who has sung of it.
This is the Ultimate Word: but can
   any express its marvellous savour?

He who has savoured it once, he
knows what joy it can give.
Kabir says : "Knowing it, the ignorant
man becomes wise, and the wise
man becomes speechless and silent,
The worshipper is utterly inebriated,
His wisdom and his detachment are
made perfect ;
He drinks from the cup of the in-
breathings and the outbreathings
of love."

There the whole sky is filled with
sound, and there that music is
made without fingers and without
strings ;
There the game of pleasure and pain
does not cease.
Kabir says : "If you merge your life
in the Ocean of Life, you will find
your life in the Supreme Land of
Bliss."

What a frenzy of ecstasy there is in

every hour! and the worshipper is
pressing out and drinking the
essence of the hours: he lives in
the life of Brahma.
I speak truth, for I have accepted truth
in life; I am now attached to
truth, I have swept all tinsel away.
Kabir says: "Thus is the worshipper
set free from fear; thus have all
errors of life and of death left
him."

There the sky is filled with music:
There it rains nectar:
There the harp-strings jingle, and there
the drums beat.
What a secret splendour is there, in
the mansion of the sky!
There no mention is made of the rising
and the setting of the sun;
In the ocean of manifestation, which is
the light of love, day and night
are felt to be one.

Joy for ever, no sorrow, no struggle!
There have I seen joy filled to the brim,
    perfection of joy;
No place for error is there.
Kabir says: "There have I witnessed
    the sport of One Bliss!"

I have known in my body the sport of
    the universe: I have escaped from
    the error of this world.
The inward and the outward are be-
    come as one sky, the Infinite and
    the finite are united: I am drunken
    with the sight of this All!
This Light of Thine fulfils the uni-
    verse: the lamp of love that burns
    on the salver of knowledge.
Kabir says: "There error cannot enter,
    and the conflict of life and death
    is felt no more."

XVIII

II. 77. *maddh ākāś āp jahān baiṭhe*

THE middle region of the sky,
  wherein the spirit dwelleth, is
  radiant with the music of light;
There, where the pure and white music
  blossoms, my Lord takes His de-
  light.
In the wondrous effulgence of each hair
  of His body, the brightness of mill-
  ions of suns and of moons is lost.
On that shore there is a city, where the
  rain of nectar pours and pours, and
  never ceases.
Kabir says: "Come, O Dharmadas!
  and see my great Lord's Durbar."

XIX

II. 20. *paramātam guru nikaṭ virājaiṉ*

O MY heart! the Supreme Spirit,
  the great Master, is near you:
  wake, oh wake!
Run to the feet of your Beloved: for

your Lord stands near to your
head.
You have slept for unnumbered ages;
this morning will you not wake?

XX

II. 22. man tu pār utar kānh jaiho

TO what shore would you cross, O
my heart? there is no traveller
before you, there is no road:
Where is the movement, where is the
rest, on that shore?
There is no water; no boat, no boat-
man, is there;
There is not so much as a rope to tow
the boat, nor a man to draw it.
No earth, no sky, no time, no thing, is
there: no shore, no ford!
There, there is neither body nor mind:
and where is the place that shall
still the thirst of the soul? You
shall find naught in that emptiness.
Be strong, and enter into your own

body: for there your foothold is
firm. Consider it well, O my
heart! go not elsewhere.

Kabir says: "Put all imaginations
away, and stand fast in that which
you are."

XXI

II. 33. *ghar ghar dīpak barai*

LAMPS burn in every house, O
blind one! and you cannot see
them.

One day your eyes shall suddenly be
opened, and you shall see: and the
fetters of death will fall from you.

There is nothing to say or to hear,
there is nothing to do: it is he
who is living, yet dead, who shall
never die again.

Because he lives in solitude, therefore
the Yogi says that his home is far
away.

Your Lord is near: yet you are climb-
ing the palm-tree to seek Him.
The Brahman priest goes from house
to house and initiates people into
faith:
Alas! the true fountain of life is beside
you, and you have set up a stone
to worship.
Kabir says: "I may never express how
sweet my Lord is. Yoga and the
telling of beads, virtue and vice —
these are naught to Him."

XXII

II. 38. *Sādho, so satgur mohi bhāwai*

O BROTHER, my heart yearns for
that true Guru, who fills the cup
of true love, and drinks of it him-
self, and offers it then to me.
He removes the veil from the eyes, and
gives the true Vision of Brahma:
He reveals the worlds in Him, and

makes me to hear the Unstruck
Music :
He shows joy and sorrow to be one :
He fills all utterance with love.
Kabir says : "Verily he has no fear,
    who has such a Guru to lead him
    to the shelter of safety !"

XXIII

II. 40.   *tinwir sāñjh kā gahirā āwai*

THE shadows of evening fall thick
    and deep, and the darkness of love
    envelops the body and the mind.
Open the window to the west, and be
    lost in the sky of love ;
Drink the sweet honey that steeps the
    petals of the lotus of the heart.
Receive the waves in your body : what
    splendour is in the region of the
    sea !
Hark ! the sounds of conches and bells
    are rising.

Kabir says: "O brother, behold! the Lord is in this vessel of my body."

XXIV

II. 48. *jis se rahani apār jagat men*

MORE than all else do I cherish at heart that love which makes me to live a limitless life in this world.

It is like the lotus, which lives in the water and blooms in the water: yet the water cannot touch its petals, they open beyond its reach.

It is like a wife, who enters the fire at the bidding of love. She burns and lets others grieve, yet never dishonours love.

This ocean of the world is hard to cross: its waters are very deep. Kabir says: "Listen to me, O Sadhu! few there are who have reached its end."

XXV

II. 45.   *Hari ne apnā āp chipāyā*

MY Lord hides Himself, and my
Lord wonderfully reveals Him-
self:

My Lord has encompassed me with
hardness, and my Lord has cast
down my limitations.

My Lord brings to me words of sorrow
and words of joy, and He Himself
heals their strife.

I will offer my body and mind to my
Lord: I will give up my life, but
never can I forget my Lord!

XXVI

II. 75.   *ōnkār siwae kōī sirjai*

ALL things are created by the Om;
The love-form is His body.

He is without form, without quality,
without decay:

Seek thou union with Him!

But that formless God takes a thousand
　　forms in the eyes of His creatures:
He is pure and indestructible,
His form is infinite and fathomless,
He dances in rapture, and waves of
　　form arise from His dance.
The body and the mind cannot contain
　　themselves, when they are touched
　　by His great joy.
He is immersed in all consciousness, all
　　joys, and all sorrows;
He has no beginning and no end;
He holds all within His bliss.

XXVII

II. 81.   satgur sōī dayā kar dīnhā

IT is the mercy of my true Guru that
　　has made me to know the un-
　　known;
I have learned from Him how to walk
　　without feet, to see without eyes,
　　to hear without ears, to drink

without mouth, to fly without
wings;
I have brought my love and my medi-
tation into the land where there
is no sun and moon, nor day and
night.
Without eating, I have tasted of the
sweetness of nectar; and without
water, I have quenched my thirst.
Where there is the response of delight,
there is the fullness of joy. Be-
fore whom can that joy be uttered?
Kabir says: "The Guru is great be-
yond words, and great is the good
fortune of the disciple."

XXVIII

II. 85. *nirguṇ āge sarguṇ nācai*

BEFORE the Unconditioned, the
Conditioned dances:
"Thou and I are one!" this trumpet
proclaims.

The Guru comes, and bows down before
the disciple:
This is the greatest of wonders.

XXIX

II. 87.   *Kabīr kab se bhaye vairāgī*

GORAKHNATH asks Kabir:
"Tell me, O Kabir, when did
your vocation begin? Where did
your love have its rise?"
Kabir answers:
"When He whose forms are manifold
had not begun His play: when
there was no Guru, and no disciple:
when the world was not spread
out: when the Supreme One was
alone —
Then I became an ascetic; then, O
Gorakh, my love was drawn to
Brahma.
Brahmā did not hold the crown on his
head; the god Vishnu was not

anointed as king; the power of
Shiva was still unborn; when I
was instructed in Yoga.

I became suddenly revealed in Benares,
    and Ramananda illumined me;
I brought with me the thirst for the
    Infinite, and I have come for the
    meeting with Him.
In simplicity will I unite with the
    Simple One; my love will surge
    up.
O Gorakh, march thou with His
    music!"

XXX

II. 95. *yā tarvar men̄ ek pakherū*

ON this tree is a bird: it dances
    in the joy of life.
None knows where it is: and who
    knows what the burden of its
    music may be?
Where the branches throw a deep

shade, there does it have its nest:
and it comes in the evening and
flies away in the morning, and says
not a word of that which it means.
None tell me of this bird that sings
within me.
It is neither coloured nor colourless: it
has neither form nor outline:
It sits in the shadow of love.
It dwells within the Unattainable, the
Infinite, and the Eternal; and no
one marks when it comes and goes.
Kabir says: "O brother Sadhu! deep
is the mystery. Let wise men seek
to know where rests that bird."

XXXI

II. 100. *niṡ din sālai ghāw*

A SORE pain troubles me day and
night, and I cannot sleep;
I long for the meeting with my Beloved,
and my father's house gives me
pleasure no more.

The gates of the sky are opened, the
    temple is revealed:
I meet my husband, and leave at His
    feet the offering of my body and
    my mind.

XXXII

II. 103. *nāco re mero man, matta hoy*

DANCE, my heart! dance to-day
    with joy.
The strains of love fill the days and
    the nights with music, and the
    world is listening to its melodies:
Mad with joy, life and death dance to
    the rhythm of this music. The
    hills and the sea and the earth
    dance. The world of man dances
    in laughter and tears.
Why put on the robe of the monk, and
    live aloof from the world in lonely
    pride?
Behold! my heart dances in the de-

light of a hundred arts; and the
Creator is well pleased.

XXXIII

II. 105. *man mast huā tab kyon bole*

WHERE is the need of words,
when love has made drunken
the heart?
I have wrapped the diamond in my
cloak; why open it again and
again?
When its load was light, the pan of the
balance went up: now it is full,
where is the need for weighing?
The swan has taken its flight to the
lake beyond the mountains; why
should it search for the pools and
ditches any more?
Your Lord dwells within you: why
need your outward eyes be opened?
Kabir says: "Listen, my brother! my
Lord, who ravishes my eyes, has
united Himself with me."

XXXIV

II. 110. *mohi tohi lāgī kaise chuṭe*

HOW could the love between Thee
and me sever?

As the leaf of the lotus abides on the
water: so thou art my Lord, and
I am Thy servant.

As the night-bird Chakor gazes all
night at the moon: so Thou art
my Lord and I am Thy servant.

From the beginning until the ending
of time, there is love between
Thee and me; and how shall such
love be extinguished?

Kabir says: "As the river enters into the
ocean, so my heart touches Thee."

XXXV

II. 113. *vālam, āwo hamāre geh re*

MY body and my mind are grieved
for the want of Thee;

O my Beloved! come to my house.

When people say I am Thy bride, I am
    ashamed; for I have not touched
    Thy heart with my heart.
Then what is this love of mine? I have
    no taste for food, I have no sleep;
    my heart is ever restless within
    doors and without.
As water is to the thirsty, so is the
    lover to the bride. Who is there
    that will carry my news to my
    Beloved?
Kabir is restless: he is dying for sight
    of Him.

XXXVI

II. 126. *jāg piyārī, ab kān sowai*

O FRIEND, awake, and sleep no
    more!
The night is over and gone, would you
    lose your day also?
Others, who have wakened, have re-
    ceived jewels;

O foolish woman! you have lost all
whilst you slept.
Your lover is wise, and you are foolish,
O woman!
You never prepared the bed of your
husband:
O mad one! you passed your time in
silly play.
Your youth was passed in vain, for you
did not know your Lord;
Wake, wake! See! your bed is empty:
He left you in the night.
Kabir says: "Only she wakes, whose
heart is pierced with the arrow
of His music."

XXXVII

I. 36. *sūr parkās, tanh rain kahān*
pāïye

WHERE is the night, when the
sun is shining? If it is night,
then the sun withdraws its light.
Where knowledge is, can ignorance en-

dure? If there be ignorance, then
knowledge must die.
If there be lust, how can love be there?
Where there is love, there is no lust.

Lay hold on your sword, and join in
the fight. Fight, O my brother,
as long as life lasts.
Strike off your enemy's head, and
there make an end of him quickly:
then come, and bow your head at
your King's Durbar.
He who is brave, never forsakes the
battle: he who flies from it is no
true fighter.
In the field of this body a great war
goes forward, against passion, an-
ger, pride, and greed:
It is in the kingdom of truth, content-
ment and purity, that this battle
is raging; and the sword that
rings forth most loudly is the
sword of His Name.

Kabir says: "When a brave knight takes the field, a host of cowards is put to flight.

It is a hard fight and a weary one, this fight of the truth-seeker: for the vow of the truth-seeker is more hard than that of the warrior, or of the widowed wife who would follow her husband.

For the warrior fights for a few hours, and the widow's struggle with death is soon ended:

But the truth-seeker's battle goes on day and night, as long as life lasts it never ceases."

XXXVIII

I. 50. *bhram kā tālā lagā mahal re*

THE lock of error shuts the gate, open it with the key of love:
Thus, by opening the door, thou shalt wake the Beloved.

Kabir says: "O brother! do not pass
by such good fortune as this."

XXXIX

I. 59.   *sādho, yạh tan ṭhāṭh tanvure kâ*

O FRIEND! this body is His lyre;
He tightens its strings, and draws
from it the melody of Brahma.
If the strings snap and the keys
slacken, then to dust must this in-
strument of dust return:
Kabir says: "None but Brahma can
evoke its melodies."

XL

I. 65.   *avadhū bhūle ko ghar lāwe*

HE is dear to me indeed who can
call back the wanderer to his
home. In the home is the true
union, in the home is enjoyment of
life: why should I forsake my
home and wander in the forest?

If Brahma helps me to realize truth, verily I will find both bondage and deliverance in home.

He is dear to me indeed who has power to dive deep into Brahma; whose mind loses itself with ease in His contemplation.

He is dear to me who knows Brahma, and can dwell on His supreme truth in meditation; and who can play the melody of the Infinite by uniting love and renunciation in life.

Kabir says: "The home is the abiding place; in the home is reality; the home helps to attain Him Who is real. So stay where you are, and all things shall come to you in time."

XLI

I. 76. *santo, sahaj samādh bhalī*

O SADHU! the simple union is the best.

Since the day when I met with my

Lord, there has been no end to
   the sport of our love.
I shut not my eyes, I close not my ears,
   I do not mortify my body;
I see with eyes open and smile, and
   behold His beauty everywhere:
I utter His Name, and whatever I see,
   it reminds me of Him; whatever
   I do, it becomes His worship.
The rising and the setting are one to
   me; all contradictions are solved.
Wherever I go, I move round Him,
All I achieve is His service:
When I lie down, I lie prostrate at His
   feet.

He is the only adorable one to me: I
   have none other.
My tongue has left off impure words,
   it sings His glory day and night:
Whether I rise or sit down, I can never
   forget Him; for the rhythm of
   His music beats in my ears.

Kabir says: "My heart is frenzied, and I disclose in my soul what is hidden. I am immersed in that one great bliss which transcends all pleasure and pain."

XLII

I. 79. *tīrath men to sab pānī hai*

THERE is nothing but water at the holy bathing places; and I know that they are useless, for I have bathed in them.

The images are all lifeless, they cannot speak; I know, for I have cried aloud to them.

The Purana and the Koran are mere words; lifting up the curtain, I have seen.

Kabir gives utterance to the words of experience; and he knows very well that all other things are untrue.

XLIII

I. 82. *pānī vic mīn piyāsī*

I LAUGH when I hear that the fish
in the water is thirsty:
You do not see that the Real is in your
home, and you wander from forest
to forest listlessly!
Here is the truth! Go where you will,
to Benares or to Mathura; if you
do not find your soul, the world is
unreal to you.

XLIV

I. 93. *gagan maṭh gaib nisān gaḍe*

THE Hidden Banner is planted in
the temple of the sky; there the
blue canopy decked with the moon
and set with bright jewels is spread.
There the light of the sun and the
moon is shining: still your mind
to silence before that splendour.

Kabir says: "He who has drunk of this
    nectar, wanders like one who is
    mad."

XLV

I. 97.   *sādho, ko hai kānh se āyo*

WHO are you, and whence do you
    come?
Where dwells that Supreme Spirit, and
    how does He have His sport with
    all created things?
The fire is in the wood; but who
    awakens it suddenly? Then it
    turns to ashes, and where goes the
    force of the fire?
The true guru teaches that He has
    neither limit nor infinitude.
Kabir says: "Brahma suits His lan-
    guage to the understanding of His
    hearer."

XLVI

I. 98.   sādho, sahajai kāyā śodho

O SADHU! purify your body in
the simple way.

As the seed is within the banyan tree,
and within the seed are the flowers,
the fruits, and the shade:

So the germ is within the body, and
within that germ is the body again.

The fire, the air, the water, the earth,
and the aether; you cannot have
these outside of Him.

O Kazi, O Pundit, consider it well:
what is there that is not in the
soul?

The water-filled pitcher is placed upon
water, it has water within and
without.

It should not be given a name, lest it
call forth the error of dualism.

Kabir says: "Listen to the Word, the
Truth, which is your essence. He

speaks the Word to Himself; and
He Himself is the Creator."

XLVII

I. 102. *tarvar ek mūl vin ṭhāḍā*

THERE is a strange tree, which
stands without roots and bears
fruits without blossoming;
It has no branches and no leaves, it is
lotus all over.
Two birds sing there; one is the Guru,
and the other the disciple:
The disciple chooses the manifold fruits
of life and tastes them, and the
Guru beholds him in joy.
What Kabir says is hard to understand:
" The bird is beyond seeking, yet it
is most clearly visible. The Form-
less is in the midst of all forms. I
sing the glory of forms."

XLVIII

I. 107. *calat mansā acal kīnhī*

I HAVE stilled my restless mind, and my heart is radiant: for in That-ness I have seen beyond That-ness, in company I have seen the Comrade Himself.

Living in bondage, I have set myself free: I have broken away from the clutch of all narrowness.

Kabir says: "I have attained the unattainable, and my heart is coloured with the colour of love."

XLIX

I. 105. *jo dīsai, so to hai nāhīn*

THAT which you see is not: and for that which is, you have no words.

Unless you see, you believe not: what is told you you cannot accept.

He who is discerning knows by the word; and the ignorant stands gaping.

Some contemplate the Formless, and
others meditate on form : but the
wise man knows that Brahma is
beyond both.

That beauty of His is not seen of the
eye : that metre of His is not heard
of the ear.

Kabir says : "He who has found both
love and renunciation never de-
scends to death."

L

I. 126.   *murali bajat akhaṇḍ sadāye*

THE flute of the Infinite is played
without ceasing, and its sound is
love :

When love renounces all limits, it
reaches truth.

How widely the fragrance spreads ! It
has no end, nothing stands in its
way.

The form of this melody is bright like

a million suns: incomparably
sounds the vina, the vina of the
notes of truth.

LI

I. 129. *sakhiyo, ham hūn bhāī vāla-
māsī*

DEAR friend, I am eager to meet
my Beloved! My youth has
flowered, and the pain of separa-
tion from Him troubles my breast.
I am wandering yet in the alleys of
knowledge without purpose, but I
have received His news in these
alleys of knowledge.
I have a letter from my Beloved: in
this letter is an unutterable mes-
sage, and now my fear of death is
done away.
Kabir says: "O my loving friend! I
have got for my gift the Deathless
One."

LII

I. 130.   sāin̠ vin dard kareje hoy

WHEN I am parted from my
Beloved, my heart is full of
misery: I have no comfort in the
day, I have no sleep in the night.
To whom shall I tell my sorrow?
The night is dark; the hours slip by.
Because my Lord is absent, I start
up and tremble with fear.
Kabir says: "Listen, my friend! there
is no other satisfaction, save in the
encounter with the Beloved."

LIII

*I. 122.   kaum muralī śabd śun ānand
bhayo*

WHAT is that flute whose music
thrills me with joy?
The flame burns without a lamp;
The lotus blossoms without a root;

Flowers bloom in clusters;
The moon-bird is devoted to the moon;
With all its heart the rain-bird longs
    for the shower of rain;
But upon whose love does the Lover
    concentrate His entire life?

LIV

I. 112. *śuntā nahī dhun kī khabar*

HAVE you not heard the tune
which the Unstruck Music is
playing? In the midst of the
chamber the harp of joy is gently
and sweetly played; and where is
the need of going without to hear
it?

If you have not drunk of the nectar of
that One Love, what boots it
though you should purge yourself
of all stains?

The Kazi is searching the words of the
Koran, and instructing others:

but if his heart be not steeped in
that love, what does it avail,
though he be a teacher of men?
The Yogi dyes his garments with red:
but if he knows naught of that
colour of love, what does it avail
though his garments be tinted?
Kabir says: "Whether I be in the
temple or the balcony, in the camp
or in the flower garden, I tell you
truly that every moment my Lord
is taking His delight in me."

LV

I. 73. *bhakti kā mārag jhīnā re*

SUBTLE is the path of love!
 Therein there is no asking and
no not-asking,
There one loses one's self at His feet,
There one is immersed in the joy of
the seeking: plunged in the deeps
of love as the fish in the water.

The lover is never slow in offering his
head for his Lord's service.
Kabir declares the secret of this love.

LVI

I. 68.   *bhāi koi satguru sant kahāwai*

HE is the real Sadhu, who can re-
veal the form of the Formless to
the vision of these eyes:
Who teaches the simple way of attain-
ing Him, that is other than rites
or ceremonies:
Who does not make you close the doors,
and hold the breath, and renounce
the world:
Who makes you perceive the Supreme
Spirit wherever the mind attaches
itself:
Who teaches you to be still in the midst
of all your activities.
Ever immersed in bliss, having no fear
in his mind, he keeps the spirit of

union in the midst of all enjoy-
ments.

The infinite dwelling of the Infinite
Being is everywhere: in earth,
water, sky, and air:
Firm as the thunderbolt, the seat of
the seeker is established above the
void.
He who is within is without: I see
Him and none else.

LVII

I. 66.   *sādho, śabd sādhnā kījai*

RECEIVE that Word from which
the Universe springeth!
That word is the Guru; I have heard
it, and become the disciple.
How many are there who know the
meaning of that word?

O Sadhu! practise that Word!
The Vedas and the Puranas proclaim it,
The world is established in it,

The Rishis and devotees speak of it:
But none knows the mystery of the
　　Word.
The householder leaves his house when
　　he hears it,
The ascetic comes back to love when
　　he hears it,
The Six Philosophies expound it,
The Spirit of Renunciation points to
　　that Word,
From that Word the world-form has
　　sprung,
That Word reveals all.
Kabir says: "But who knows whence
　　the Word cometh?"

LVIII

I. 63.　*pīle pyālā, ho matwālā*

EMPTY the Cup! O be drunken!
　　Drink the divine nectar of His
Name!
Kabir says: "Listen to me, dear Sadhu!

From the sole of the foot to the crown
of the head this mind is filled with
poison."

LIX

I. 52.   *khasm na cīnhai bāwarī*

O MAN, if thou dost not know thine
own Lord, whereof art thou so
proud?
Put thy cleverness away: mere words
shall never unite thee to Him.
Do not deceive thyself with the witness
of the Scriptures:
Love is something other than this, and
he who has sought it truly has
found it.

LX

I. 56.   *sukh sindh kī sair kā*

THE savour of wandering in the
ocean of deathless life has rid
me of all my asking:

As the tree is in the seed, so all diseases
are in this asking.

LXI

I. 48.   *sukh sāgar men̲ āīke*

WHEN at last you are come to the
ocean of happiness, do not go
back thirsty.

Wake, foolish man! for Death stalks
you.   Here is pure water before
you; drink it at every breath.

Do not follow the mirage on foot, but
thirst for the nectar;

Dhruva, Prahlad, and Shukadeva have
drunk of it, and also Raidas has
tasted it:

The saints are drunk with love, their
thirst is for love.

Kabir says: "Listen to me, brother!
The nest of fear is broken.

Not for a moment have you come face
to face with the world:

You are weaving your bondage of
    falsehood, your words are full of
    deception:
With the load of desires which you hold
    on your head, how can you be
    light?"
Kabir says: "Keep within you truth,
    detachment, and love."

LXII

I. 35. *satī ko kaun śikhāwtā hai*

WHO has ever taught the widowed
    wife to burn herself on the pyre
of her dead husband?
And who has ever taught love to find
    bliss in renunciation?

LXIII

I. 39. *are man, dhīraj kāhe na dharai*

WHY so impatient, my heart?
    He who watches over birds,
beasts, and insects,

He who cared for you whilst you were
    yet in your mother's womb,
Shall He not care for you now that you
    are come forth?
Oh my heart, how could you turn from
    the smile of your Lord and wander
    so far from Him?
You have left your Beloved and are
    thinking of others: and this is
    why all your work is in vain.

LXIV

I. 117. *sāīn se lagan kaṭhin hai, bhāī*

HOW hard it is to meet my Lord!
    The rain-bird wails in thirst for
    the rain: almost she dies of her
    longing, yet she would have none
    other water than the rain.
Drawn by the love of music, the deer
    moves forward: she dies as she
    listens to the music, yet she shrinks
    not in fear.

The widowed wife sits by the body of
her dead husband: she is not
afraid of the fire.
Put away all fear for this poor body.

LXV

I. 22. *jab main bhūlā, re bhāī*

O BROTHER! when I was for-
getful, my true Guru showed me
the Way.
Then I left off all rites and ceremonies,
I bathed no more in the holy
water:
Then I learned that it was I alone who
was mad, and the whole world
beside me was sane; and I had
disturbed these wise people.
From that time forth I knew no more
how to roll in the dust in obei-
sance:
I do not ring the temple bell:
I do not set the idol on its throne:

I do not worship the image with flowers.

It is not the austerities that mortify the flesh which are pleasing to the Lord,

When you leave off your clothes and kill your senses, you do not please the Lord:

The man who is kind and who practises righteousness, who remains passive amidst the affairs of the world, who considers all creatures on earth as his own self,

He attains the Immortal Being, the true God is ever with him.

Kabir says: "He attains the true Name whose words are pure, and who is free from pride and conceit."

LXVI

I. 20. *man na raṅgāye*

THE Yogi dyes his garments, instead of dyeing his mind in the colours of love:

He sits within the temple of the Lord,
leaving Brahma to worship a stone.

He pierces holes in his ears, he has a
great beard and matted locks, he
looks like a goat:

He goes forth into the wilderness, kill-
ing all his desires, and turns him-
self into an eunuch:

He shaves his head and dyes his gar-
ments; he reads the Gita and be-
comes a mighty talker.

Kabir says: "You are going to the
doors of death, bound hand and
foot!"

LXVII

I. 9. *nā jāne sāhab kaisā hai*

I DO not know what manner of God
is mine.

The Mullah cries aloud to Him: and
why? Is your Lord deaf? The
subtle anklets that ring on the

feet of an insect when it moves are heard of Him.

Tell your beads, paint your forehead with the mark of your God, and wear matted locks long and showy: but a deadly weapon is in your heart, and how shall you have God?

LXVIII

III. 102.   *ham se rahā na jāy*

I HEAR the melody of His flute, and I cannot contain myself:

The flower blooms, though it is not spring; and already the bee has received its invitation.

The sky roars and the lightning flashes, the waves arise in my heart,

The rain falls; and my heart longs for my Lord.

Where the rhythm of the world rises and falls, thither my heart has reached:

There the hidden banners are fluttering
    in the air.
Kabir says: "My heart is dying,
    though it lives."

LXIX

III. 2. *jo khodā masjid vasat hai*

IF God be within the mosque, then
    to whom does this world belong?
If Ram be within the image which you
    find upon your pilgrimage, then
    who is there to know what happens
    without?
Hari is in the East: Allah is in the
    West. Look within your heart,
    for there you will find both Karim
    and Ram;
All the men and women of the world
    are His living forms.
Kabir is the child of Allah and of Ram:
    He is my Guru, He is my Pir.

LXX

III. 9.   *śīl santosh sadā samadṛishṭi*

HE who is meek and contented, he
who has an equal vision, whose
mind is filled with the fullness of
acceptance and of rest;

He who has seen Him and touched
Him, he is freed from all fear and
trouble.

To him the perpetual thought of God
is like sandal paste smeared on
the body, to him nothing else is
delight:

His work and his rest are filled with
music: he sheds abroad the radi-
ance of love.

Kabir says: "Touch His feet, who is
one and indivisible, immutable
and peaceful; who fills all vessels
to the brim with joy, and whose
form is love."

LXXI

III. 13.   *sādh saṅgat pītam*

GO thou to the company of the
good, where the Beloved One
has His dwelling place:
Take all thy thoughts and love and
instruction from thence.
Let that assembly be burnt to ashes
where His Name is not spoken!
Tell me, how couldst thou hold a
wedding-feast, if the bridegroom
himself were not there?
Waver no more, think only of the Be-
loved;
Set not thy heart on the worship of
other gods, there is no worth in
the worship of other masters.
Kabir deliberates and says: "Thus
thou shalt never find the Be-
loved!"

LXXII

III. 26. *tor hīrā hirāilwā kīcad men*

THE jewel is lost in the mud, and
     all are seeking for it;
Some look for it in the east, and some
     in the west; some in the water
     and some amongst stones.
But the servant Kabir has appraised it
     at its true value, and has wrapped
     it with care in the end of the
     mantle of his heart.

LXXIII

III. 26. *āyau din gaune kā ho*

THE palanquin came to take me
     away to my husband's home,
     and it sent through my heart a
     thrill of joy;
But the bearers have brought me into
     the lonely forest, where I have no
     one of my own.

O bearers, I entreat you by your feet,
    wait but a moment longer : let me
    go back to my kinsmen and friends,
    and take my leave of them.
The servant Kabir sings : "O Sadhu !
    finish your buying and selling,
    have done with your good and
    your bad : for there are no mar-
    kets and no shops in the land to
    which you go."

LXXIV

III. 30. ˙ *are dil, prem nagar kā ant na*
               pāyā

O MY heart ! you have not known
    all the secrets of this city of
    love : in ignorance you came, and
    in ignorance you return.
O my friend, what have you done with
    this life ? You have taken on your
    head the burden heavy with stones,
    and who is to lighten it for you ?

Your Friend stands on the other shore,
    but you never think in your mind
    how you may meet with Him:
The boat is broken, and yet you sit
    ever upon the bank; and thus you
    are beaten to no purpose by the
    waves.
The servant Kabir asks you to con-
    sider; who is there that shall be-
    friend you at the last?
You are alone, you have no companion:
    you will suffer the consequences
    of your own deeds.

LXXV

III. 55. *ved kahe sarguṇ ke āge*

THE Vedas say that the Uncondi-
tioned stands beyond the world
of Conditions.
O woman, what does it avail thee to
    dispute whether He is beyond all
    or in all?

See thou everything as thine own
dwelling place : the mist of pleas-
ure and pain can never spread there.
There Brahma is revealed day and
night : there light is His garment,
light is His seat, light rests on thy
head.
Kabir says : "The Master, who is true,
He is all light."

LXXVI

III. 48. *tū surat nain nihār*

OPEN your eyes of love, and see
Him who pervades this world !
consider it well, and know that
this is your own country.
When you meet the true Guru, He will
awaken your heart ;
He will tell you the secret of love and
detachment, and then you will
know indeed that He transcends
this universe.

This world is the City of Truth, its
    maze of paths enchants the heart :
We can reach the goal without crossing
    the road, such is the sport unend-
    ing.
Where the ring of manifold joys ever
    dances about Him, there is the
    sport of Eternal Bliss.
When we know this, then all our re-
    ceiving and renouncing is over ;
Thenceforth the heat of having shall
    never scorch us more.

He is the Ultimate Rest unbounded :
He has spread His form of love through-
    out all the world.
From that Ray which is Truth, streams
    of new forms are perpetually spring-
    ing : and He pervades those forms.
All the gardens and groves and bowers
    are abounding with blossom ; and
    the air breaks forth into ripples
    of joy.

There the swan plays a wonderful game,
There the Unstruck Music eddies
    around the Infinite One;
There in the midst the Throne of the
    Unheld is shining, whereon the
    great Being sits —
Millions of suns are shamed by the
    radiance of a single hair of His
    body.
On the harp of the road what true
    melodies are being sounded! and
    its notes pierce the heart:
There the Eternal Fountain is playing
    its endless life-streams of birth
    and death.
They call Him Emptiness who is the
    Truth of truths, in Whom all
    truths are stored!

There within Him creation goes for-
    ward, which is beyond all philoso-
    phy; for philosophy cannot attain
    to Him:

There is an endless world, O my
Brother! and there is the Name-
less Being, of whom naught can
be said.

Only he knows it who has reached that
region: it is other than all that
is heard and said.

No form, no body, no length, no
breadth is seen there: how can I
tell you that which it is?

He comes to the Path of the Infinite
on whom the grace of the Lord
descends: he is freed from births
and deaths who attains to Him.

Kabir says: "It cannot be told by the
words of the mouth, it cannot be
written on paper:

It is like a dumb person who tastes a
sweet thing — how shall it be ex-
plained?"

LXXVII

III. 60.   *cal haṃsā wā deś jahān*

O MY heart! let us go to that
country where dwells the Be-
loved, the ravisher of my heart!

There Love is filling her pitcher from
the well, yet she has no rope where-
with to draw water;

There the clouds do not cover the sky,
yet the rain falls down in gentle
showers:

O bodiless one! do not sit on your
doorstep; go forth and bathe
yourself in that rain!

There it is ever moonlight and never
dark; and who speaks of one sun
only? that land is illuminate with
the rays of a million suns.

LXXVIII

III. 63.   kahain Kabīr, śuno ho sādho

KABIR says: "O Sadhu! hear
my deathless words. If you
want your own good, examine and
consider them well.

You have estranged yourself from the
Creator, of whom you have sprung:
you have lost your reason, you
have bought death.

All doctrines and all teachings are
sprung from Him, from Him they
grow: know this for certain, and
have no fear.

Hear from me the tidings of this great
truth!

Whose name do you sing, and on whom
do you meditate? O, come forth
from this entanglement!

He dwells at the heart of all things, so
why take refuge in empty desola-
tion?

If you place the Guru at a distance
from you, then it is but the dis-
tance that you honour:

If indeed the Master be far away, then
who is it else that is creating this
world?

When you think that He is not here,
then you wander further and
further away, and seek Him in
vain with tears.

Where He is far off, there He is un-
attainable: where He is near, He
is very bliss.

Kabir says: "Lest His servant should
suffer pain He pervades him
through and through."

Know yourself then, O Kabir; for He
is in you from head to foot.

Sing with gladness, and keep your seat
unmoved within your heart.

LXXIX

III. 66. *nā main dharmī nahīn adharmī*

I AM neither pious nor ungodly,
  I live neither by law nor by sense,
I am neither a speaker nor hearer,
I am neither a servant nor master,
I am neither bond nor free,
I am neither detached nor attached.
I am far from none: I am near to none.
I shall go neither to hell nor to heaven.
I do all works; yet I am apart from
  all works.
Few comprehend my meaning: he who
  can comprehend it, he sits un-
  moved.
Kabir seeks neither to establish nor to
  destroy.

LXXX

III. 69. *satta nām hai sab ten̲ nyārā*

THE true Name is like none other
name!

The distinction of the Conditioned
from the Unconditioned is but a
word:

The Unconditioned is the seed, the
Conditioned is the flower and the
fruit.

Knowledge is the branch, and the
Name is the root.

Look, and see where the root is: hap-
piness shall be yours when you
come to the root.

The root will lead you to the branch,
the leaf, the flower, and the fruit:

It is the encounter with the Lord, it is
the attainment of bliss, it is the
reconciliation of the Conditioned
and the Unconditioned.

LXXXI

III. 74.   pratham ek jo āpai āp

IN the beginning was He alone, sufficient unto Himself: the formless, colourless, and unconditioned Being.

Then was there neither beginning, middle, nor end;

Then were no eyes, no darkness, no light;

Then were no ground, air, nor sky; no fire, water, nor earth; no rivers like the Ganges and the Jumna, no seas, oceans, and waves.

Then was neither vice nor virtue; scriptures there were not, as the Vedas and Puranas, nor as the Koran.

Kabir ponders in his mind and says, "Then was there no activity: the Supreme Being remained merged in the unknown depths of His own self."

The Guru neither eats nor drinks,
    neither lives nor dies:
Neither has He form, line, colour, nor
    vesture.
He who has neither caste nor clan nor
    anything else — how may I de-
    scribe His glory?
He has neither form nor formlessness,
He has no name,
He has neither colour nor colourless-
    ness,
He has no dwelling-place.

LXXXII

III. 76. *kahain̲ Kabīr vicār ke*

KABIR ponders and says: "He
who has neither caste nor coun-
try, who is formless and without
quality, fills all space."
The Creator brought into being the
Game of Joy: and from the word
Om the Creation sprang.

The earth is His joy; His joy is the
sky;
His joy is the flashing of the sun and
the moon;
His joy is the beginning, the middle,
and the end;
His joy is eyes, darkness, and light.
Oceans and waves are His joy: His
joy the Sarasvati, the Jumna, and
the Ganges.
The Guru is One: and life and death,
union and separation, are all His
plays of joy!
His play the land and water, the whole
universe!
His play the earth and the sky!
In play is the Creation spread out, in
play it is established. The whole
world, says Kabir, rests in His
play, yet still the Player remains
unknown.

LXXXIII

III. 84.   *jhī jhī jantar bājai*

THE harp gives forth murmurous
music; and the dance goes on
without hands and feet.
It is played without fingers, it is heard
without ears: for He is the ear,
and He is the listener.
The gate is locked, but within there is
fragrance: and there the meeting
is seen of none.
The wise shall understand it.

LXXXIV

III. 89.   *mor phakīrwā māṅgi jāy*

THE Beggar goes a-begging, but
I could not even catch sight of
Him:
And what shall I beg of the Beggar?
He gives without my asking.
Kabir says: "I am His own: now let
that befall which may befall!"

LXXXV

III. 90.   *naihar se jiyarā phāṭ re*

MY heart cries aloud for the house
   of my lover; the open road and
the shelter of a roof are all one to
her who has lost the city of her
husband.
My heart finds no joy in anything: my
   mind and my body are distraught.
His palace has a million gates, but there
   is a vast ocean between it and me:
How shall I cross it, O friend? for end-
   less is the outstretching of the path.

How wondrously this lyre is wrought!
   When its strings are rightly strung,
   it maddens the heart: but when
   the keys are broken and the strings
   are loosened, none regard it more.
I tell my parents with laughter that I
   must go to my Lord in the
   morning;

They are angry, for they do not want
me to go, and they say: "She
thinks she has gained such do-
minion over her husband that she
can have whatsoever she wishes;
and therefore she is impatient to go
to him."

Dear friend, lift my veil lightly now;
for this is the night of love.

Kabir says: "Listen to me! My heart
is eager to meet my lover: I lie
sleepless upon my bed. Remem-
ber me early in the morning!"

LXXXVI

III. 96. *jīv mahal men̄ Śiv pahunwā*

SERVE your God, who has come
into this temple of life!

Do not act the part of a madman, for
the night is thickening fast.

He has awaited me for countless ages,

for love of me He has lost His
    heart:
Yet I did not know the bliss that was
    so near to me, for my love was not
    yet awake.
But now, my Lover has made known
    to me the meaning of the note that
    struck my ear:
Now, my good fortune is come.
Kabir says: "Behold! how great is
    my good fortune! I have received
    the unending caress of my Be-
    loved!"

LXXXVII

I. 71. *gagan ghaṭā ghaharānī, sādho*

CLOUDS thicken in the sky! O,
    listen to the deep voice of their
    roaring;
The rain comes from the east with its
    monotonous murmur.
Take care of the fences and boundaries

of your fields, lest the rains over-
flow them;
Prepare the soil of deliverance, and let
the creepers of love and renuncia-
tion be soaked in this shower.
It is the prudent farmer who will bring
his harvest home; he shall fill
both his vessels, and feed both
the wise men and the saints.

LXXXVIII

III. 118. *āj din ke main jāun balihārī*

THIS day is dear to me above all
other days, for to-day the Be-
loved Lord is a guest in my house;
My chamber and my courtyard are
beautiful with His presence.
My longings sing His Name, and they
are become lost in His great
beauty:
I wash His feet, and I look upon His
Face; and I lay before Him as an

offering my body, my mind, and
all that I have.

What a day of gladness is that day in
which my Beloved, who is my
treasure, comes to my house!

All evils fly from my heart when I see
my Lord.

"My love has touched Him; my heart
is longing for the Name which is
Truth."

Thus sings Kabir, the servant of all
servants.

LXXXIX

I. 100.   *kōī śuntā hai jñānī rāg gagan
men*

IS there any wise man who will listen
to that solemn music which arises
in the sky?

For He, the Source of all music, makes
all vessels full fraught, and rests in
fullness Himself.

He who is in the body is ever athirst,
 for he pursues that which is in part:
But ever there wells forth deeper and
 deeper the sound "He is this —
 this is He"; fusing love and re-
 nunciation into one.
Kabir says: "O brother! that is the
 Primal Word."

XC

I. 108. *main kā se būjhaun*

TO whom shall I go to learn about
my Beloved?
Kabir says: "As you never may find
 the forest if you ignore the tree, so
 He may never be found in abstrac-
 tions."

XCI

III. 12. *saṃskirit bhāshā paḍhi līnhā*

I HAVE learned the Sanskrit lan-
guage, so let all men call me wise:
But where is the use of this, when I

am floating adrift, and parched
　　with thirst, and burning with the
　　heat of desire?
To no purpose do you bear on your
　　head this load of pride and vanity.
Kabir says: "Lay it down in the dust,
　　and go forth to meet the Beloved.
　　Address Him as your Lord."

XCII

III. 110. *carkhā calai surat virahin kā*

THE woman who is parted from her
　　lover spins at the spinning wheel.
The city of the body arises in its
　　beauty; and within it the palace
　　of the mind has been built.
The wheel of love revolves in the sky,
　　and the seat is made of the jewels
　　of knowledge:
What subtle threads the woman weaves,
　　and makes them fine with love
　　and reverence!

Kabir says: "I am weaving the gar-
land of day and night. When
my Lover comes and touches me
with His feet, I shall offer Him my
tears."

XCIII

III. 111. *koṭīn bhānu candra tārāgaṇ*

BENEATH the great umbrella of
my King millions of suns and
moons and stars are shining!
He is the Mind within my mind: He
is the Eye within mine eye.
Ah, could my mind and eyes be one!
Could my love but reach to my
Lover! Could but the fiery heat
of my heart be cooled!
Kabir says: "When you unite love
with the Lover, then you have
love's perfection."

XCIV

I. 92. *avadhū begam deś hamārā*

O SADHU! my land is a sorrow-
less land.

I cry aloud to all, to the king and
the beggar, the emperor and the
fakir —

Whosoever seeks for shelter in the
Highest, let all come and settle
in my land!

Let the weary come and lay his burdens
here!

So live here, my brother, that you may
cross with ease to that other shore.

It is a land without earth or sky, with-
out moon or stars;

For only the radiance of Truth shines
in my Lord's Durbar.

Kabir says: "O beloved brother!
naught is essential save Truth."

XCV

I. 109. *sāīn ke saṅgat sāsur āī*

I CAME with my Lord to my Lord's home: but I lived not with Him and I tasted Him not, and my youth passed away like a dream.

On my wedding night my women-friends sang in chorus, and I was anointed with the unguents of pleasure and pain:

But when the ceremony was over, I left my Lord and came away, and my kinsman tried to console me upon the road.

Kabir says, "I shall go to my Lord's house with my love at my side; then shall I sound the trumpet of triumph!"

XCVI

I. 75.   *samajh dekh man mīt piyarwā*

O FRIEND, dear heart of mine,
      think well! if you love indeed,
   then why do you sleep?
If you have found Him, then give
   yourself utterly, and take Him to
   you.
Why do you loose Him again and
   again?
If the deep sleep of rest has come to
   your eyes, why waste your time
   making the bed and arranging
   the pillows?
Kabir says: "I tell you the ways of
   love! Even though the head itself
   must be given, why should you
   weep over it?"

XCVII

II. 90.   *sāhab ham men, sāhab tum men*

THE Lord is in me, the Lord is in
you, as life is in every seed. O
servant ! put false pride away, and
seek for Him within you.
A million suns are ablaze with light,
The sea of blue spreads in the sky,
The fever of life is stilled, and all stains
are washed away; when I sit in
the midst of that world.

Hark to the unstruck bells and drums !
Take your delight in love !
Rains pour down without water, and
the rivers are streams of light.
One Love it is that pervades the whole
world, few there are who know it
fully :
They are blind who hope to see it by
the light of reason, that reason
which is the cause of separation —
The House of Reason is very far away !

How blessed is Kabir, that amidst this
great joy he sings within his own
vessel.
It is the music of the meeting of soul
with soul;
It is the music of the forgetting of
sorrows;
It is the music that transcends all com-
ing in and all going forth.

XCVIII

II. 98.   *ṛitu phāgun niyaṛānī*

THE month of March draws near: ah,
who will unite me to my Lover?
How shall I find words for the beauty
of my Beloved?   For He is merged
in all beauty.
His colour is in all the pictures of the
world, and it bewitches the body
and the mind.
Those who know this, know what is
this unutterable play of the Spring.

Kabir says: "Listen to me, brother!
    there are not many who have
    found this out."

XCIX

II. 111.   Nārad, pyār so antar nāhī

OH Narad! I know that my Lover
    cannot be far:
When my Lover wakes, I wake; when
    He sleeps, I sleep.
He is destroyed at the root who gives
    pain to my Beloved.
Where they sing His praise, there I
    live;
When He moves, I walk before Him:
    my heart yearns for my Beloved.
The infinite pilgrimage lies at His
    feet, a million devotees are seated
    there.
Kabir says: "The Lover Himself re-
    veals the glory of true love."

C

II. 122.   *kōī prem kī peṅg jhulāo re*

HANG up the swing of love to-day!
    Hang the body and the mind
    between the arms of the Beloved,
    in the ecstasy of love's joy:
Bring the tearful streams of the rainy
    clouds to your eyes, and cover
    your heart with the shadow of
    darkness:
Bring your face nearer to His ear, and
    speak of the deepest longings of
    your heart.
Kabir says: "Listen to me, brother!
    bring the vision of the Beloved in
    your heart."